101 Things You Didn't Know About The Royal Love Birds

by

TALBOT CHURCH

'The Man The Royals Trust'

Pan Books London and Sydney

THE AUTHOR

Talbot Church was born in India where his father was a serving officer in the army. The family moved to England in 1949 and Church completed his education at King's College, Canterbury.

On leaving school, he joined the Royal College of Heralds and in 1955 was offered a job in the Royal Household, where he worked in various departments, ending up as assistant Press Secretary to His Royal Highness the Duke of Edinburgh. After several happy years in royal employment, he left the Palace to write *The Professionals – A Personal View of the Royals at Work.*

Now a freelance author and journalist, he has contributed to *Majesty, Illustrated London News* and the *Field,* and was Special Court Correspondent to *The Times* from 1972 to 1981. His other books include *The Country Life Book of Royal Residences, India – The British Heritage* and *Burke's Royal Wedding.*

A privileged royal insider, Talbot Church has accompanied the Queen on three Commonwealth tours and is currently working on *God Bless You, Ma'am,* a series for BBC Radio Four.

First published in 1986 by Pan Books Ltd,
Cavaye Place, London SW10 9PG
© 1986 Talbot Church
ISBN 0 330 297 32 5
Filmset by SX Composing Ltd, Rayleigh, Essex
Printed in Great Britain by
Cox and Wyman Ltd, Reading

Acknowledgements

The author gratefully acknowledges the help, witting or unwitting, of Fleet Street's royal trail-blazers James Whitaker, Kenneth Rose, Freddie Reed MBE, Sharon Ring, Nigel Dempster, Helen Cathcart, Sir Alastair Burnet, and Graham and Heather Fisher; of Palace watcher Deidre Quinn, who provided a valuable historical perspective; of Michael Shea, Press Secretary of the Queen, and of many other royal employees, both 'senior' and 'junior'; and of Tony Holden, who checked the manuscript for tone and balance.

Finally, I would like to acknowledge a personal debt to His Royal Highness Prince Andrew and Miss Sarah Ferguson for the many hours of informal, off-the-record interviews that formed the basis of this book.

Talbot Church
Kensington, London.

June, 1986.

At the moment of Prince Andrew's birth, his father, the Duke of Edinburgh, was playing squash with his Private Secretary. Because of prior commitments, he was only able to meet his new son some three days after the birth.

· Philip has only attended the birth of one of his children, Charles. His first comment on that occasion was said to have been, 'Hullo, Batears'! His comments on seeing Prince Andrew are not on record.

Roly-poly *Tatler* astrologer Poppé Folly says, 'In many ways the Sailor Prince is a typical Sagittarian – big, boisterous, essentially good-natured and affectionate. Sagittarians tend to charge at life, a bit like a bull in the proverbial china shop. A surprising number of Australians are Sagittarians. I'm Aries myself.'

Prince Andrew's birth created an important historical precedent. It was the first royal lying-in at which the Home Secretary was not obliged to be present. It was no coincidence that the Home Secretary at the time was the ill-fated Henry 'Don't Drink and Drive' Brooke.

Flame-haired Fergie was born on 15 October 1959 at a private nursing home in Welbeck Street, in the heart of London's fashionable West End. Beer cost a mere 1/3*d.* at the time and Joe Brown and the Bruvvers were top of the charts with 'Picture of You'.

According to an expert at the Royal College of Astronomy, star-struck Fergie is 'A typical lively Libran. Strong-willed, single-minded, but with an irrepressible sense of fun. Librans make excellent contestants on game shows. Jeremy Beadle is a typical Libran.'

Fergie's background makes her eminently suitable to be a royal sweetheart. Her family is descended from Charles II (though paradoxically not from Charles I) and her father, Major Ron Ferguson, is a first cousin of Princess Alice, Duchess of Gloucester, widow of the Queen's uncle. 'Her ancestry is impeccable,' says Harold Brooks-Baker, *Burke's Peerage* publishing director, 'in many ways better than Prince Andrew's. As non-royals go, you can't get much royaler than Miss Ferguson.'

Another ducking? Non-swimmer Andy, thrown into a lake by his father at the age of two, about to receive more encouragement from Her Majesty. He has never overcome his lifelong fear of water.

Tearaway toddler Sarah and her sister Jane were such a handful that no less than *six* nannies came and left the Ferguson household between 1959 and 1965. 'Jane was a right little tartar,' remembers a Ferguson nanny, now retired from service, 'but that Sarah! Her mother told me she was a bit of a character when I arrived but I called her a few other things in my time, I can tell you!'

Yet her days as a naughty nipper gave young Sarah an independent streak. She could walk by the time she was eleven months, was toilet trained at eighteen months and was known to make her own breakfasts at the ripe old age of three!

So I'm-in-charge Fergie started as she meant to go on – in control!

Of all the Queen's much-loved children, Andrew is the only one not to have been given a traditional royal christian name. While his other names – Albert Christian Edward – all have time-honoured royal precedents, 'Andrew' has never been used previously.

Predictably, this break with protocol was the work of Prince Philip. The Prince was looking for a suitable memorial to his favourite gundog, Andrew, that had recently died after a short illness.

Royal nanny Margaret Bath, who assisted at Prince Andrew's birth in 1960, remembers him as a particularly affectionate child, who never cried – not even at his christening. 'He was active and high-spirited. Always on the go, like a great, big puppy. He was always going and having little accidents, but he'd just pick himself up and carry on. Once he fell out of a willow tree but he didn't make a murmur. He just picked himself up and toddled off, calm as you like. He *never* cried. I think he was the very bravest of my babies.'

Everybody who knew him said the young prince had an instinctive love of life, yet he had one abiding fear as a child – water. To teach him to swim, Prince Philip – very much the traditionalist of the family – threw him into a lake at the age of two. The royal toddler sank like a stone. To this day Andrew has a love/hate relationship with water and, say royal insiders, with Prince Philip. He has never learnt to swim and later joined the Navy, rather than his first choice the Army, to overcome this fear and, according to a source close to the Palace, to please his father.

His relationship with his mother, her Majesty, was similarly ambivalent, according to his first governess, Miss Joan Pringle. They were close at first, but he seemed to resent the arrival on the scene of the baby Prince Edward, always a little charmer, and for a whole year he refused to speak. 'I can't be doing with amateur psychology,' Miss Pringle says today, 'but I think that as the middle son Prince Andrew rather felt himself to be in no man's land. Her Majesty is known to be thrifty and her insistence that Andrew wear all Charles' hand-me-downs, followed by the arrival of Edward, rather threatened Andrew's sense of identity. But he never complained and he never cried.'

By the age of six, Fergie was quite a water-baby – with courage to match. Once, while out riding near her father's Hampshire estate, she saw a young mongrel dog apparently drowning in the nearby River Test. Disregarding her own safety, the plucky Princess-to-be dismounted and plunged into the swirling waters to drag the petrified puppy to safety.

Fact: The dog's grateful owner, a farm worker, renamed it 'Fergie'.

A cheerful, sunny-natured girl, Fergie had a perfectly normal childhood, growing up on her father's £2,000,000 estate in the pretty Hampshire village of Dummer and mixing with the Royal Family from the age of six months. She first met Prince Andrew at the age of four on the polo ground at Windsor. Whether the love-birds-to-be hit it off history does not, alas, record!

Chinese astrologer Barry Fantoni predicted in 1984 that Prince Andrew – born in the year of the Tiger – would one day marry a Rat or a Horse. The former satirist got it wrong – Fergie is a Turkey.

Prince Andrew fondly remembers the occasions when his father would visit the nursery at bedtime and treat the young princes to a spirited reading from one of his favourite children's classics – they included *Kim, Mr Jorrocks' Hunting Tour* and *Ben Hur*.

Before they went to bed, the boys would be tested on what they had just heard, with the result that, to this day, Andrew is able to give a word-perfect recitation of *Little Black Sambo*.

The little Prince hated cruelty. His sister Anne, who was a keen shot from the age of seven and liked nothing better than to stalk rabbits round the royal estates with one of her father's guns, had a family of ferrets, which she called after various Socialist politicians – Wilson, Foot, Crossman, Jenkins etc. She kept them in a tool box in the royal bicycle shed in conditions that offended the young Andrew's sense of fair play. One day he released them, whereupon Crossman bit one of Her Majesty's corgis, an old favourite called Winnie, giving it a septic ear. Andrew was duly carpeted by his father but he never apologized to Anne.

The family whose memories are our memories, whose big days are our big days – the Royals relax after dinner at Sandringham in 1969. While the rest of his family are in reflective mood, archer Andy wants to be up and at 'em!

Because she thought her parents wanted a son (Major Ferguson and his first wife, Susan, already had a lovely daughter, Jane), freckle-faced Fergie played the tomboy at her first school, Daneshill, in Basingstoke. At the age of nine, the fiercely independent little girl felt she wasn't getting anywhere and decided to run away. She borrowed sixpence from underneath a milk bottle, bought a platform ticket at Basingstoke Station and stowed away in a goods van full of cattle. She got off the train at Exeter, where she tried to get a job as a vet. The local police wanted to send her home in a police car, but Sarah insisted on borrowing the train-fare and returning home unescorted.

Fact: The Ferguson family motto is Full Steam Ahead.

Like thousands of other girls of her age, the young Fergie was pony-mad and was never happier than when riding around her father's estate on one of her ponies.

She was well-known in the local pony club and won several rosettes at shows and gymkhanas. Unlike many of her friends, she was never 'blooded' while hunting with her local pack, the VWH Hunt – something which, according to friends, she has always slightly regretted.

Intrepid pony-clubber Fergie still bears a small scar five inches above her knee caused by a riding accident when she was seven.

While not sharing the family enthusiasm for all things equestrian, Andrew is himself no stranger to the saddle. Until the age of thirteen, he would hunt regularly in Leicestershire, where he acquired a considerable reputation for dash and daring beyond his years. He was 'quite a little tearaway', according to Charlie Paget, at the time a hunt servant with the ultra-smart Pytchley hounds.

'We used to have a lot of youngsters out with us in those days,' remembers Charlie, 'and some of them were good little riders and all. But I can honestly say that none of them went like Prince Andrew. Over the biggest country – walls, banks, timber, crashing through five-bar gates – he'd be in the thick of it. He scared the life out of us regulars because he was no horseman – he was completely out of control most of the time. But we had to laugh – this little tike, bouncing up and down like a sack of potatoes, hollerin' like a bloomin' red Indian!'

In fact, the tearaway toddler was 'a bit of a menace', according to Charlie. 'I've forgotten how many time he overran the hounds,' he says. 'Once he actually cannoned into the master, knocking him clean out of the saddle – but by jove he used to have a go!'

After Andrew's beloved pony, Goldie, broke a leg and had to be destroyed, the inconsolable prince lost interest in riding and these days he only returns to the saddle for state occasions.

As a boy, Prince Andrew would dread his father's shooting parties at Sandringham and Balmoral. It was a standing joke among the royals that, for days after a particularly successful shoot, Andrew would refuse to eat meat. Eventually his father put his foot down and forbade the kitchen staff from giving him anything else but pheasant. The rebellious Prince soon recovered his appetite!

The first occasion that Andrew was a 'gun' at a formal shoot was in 1971. A schoolfriend who was staying with the Prince at Balmoral recalls that it was a nerve-wracking occasion for him.

'In those days, Andy was rather odd about shooting,' he recalls. 'He just didn't like killing things. I was down the line from him but, as the beaters came towards us, I could tell that he wasn't enjoying himself. Whenever a beater cried "Over!", he'd just blast away in the general direction of the birds. The funny thing was that he actually got one – a total fluke and it rather shook him up, as it happens. But later that evening his father brought out the champagne and Andy cheered up a bit. He's never really looked back since then.'

Unlike the rest of the family, Andrew took the news of Prince Charles's decision to give up shooting with equanimity. The brother whose prowess on moor and heathland he had once envied, now gave him the magnificent Purdey 12-bore shotgun once owned by Edward VIII. The wheel had come full circle.

Fergie was never one to stand on the sidelines. Taken by her mother to a pantomime at Salisbury Playhouse, her desire to join in got the better of her. As the Big Bad Wolf, played by Cardew Robinson, began to menace Bonnie Langford as Little Red Riding Hood, six-year-old Sarah climbed on the stage, punched Mr Robinson and told him he should be ashamed of himself!

The young Andy's favourite games were Commando, Contraband and *Donner und Blitzen*. To this day, he is an avid collector of all types of military wargames and the most treasured book in his library is *The Complete Illustrated Book of Sandhurst Wargames*.

In 1973, Fergie was sent to Hurst Lodge, a theatrical school in Sunningdale, which had been started after World War II by movie-actor Leslie Howard's sister, Doris Stainer. Major Ferguson and his lovely wife Jane hoped that ballet and acting classes would smooth away some of the rough edges from their high-spirited daughter, but contemporaries remember her as 'always charging about, full of infectious enthusiasm. She was a madcap who stirred up fun wherever she went!'

In an exclusive off-the-record interview, Fergie's head-mistress at the time Miss Edith Pilgrim told me, 'Sarah certainly had a mind of her own and, though by no means academic, she was basically sound. She won a school poetry prize with a little verse that I've kept to this day. It goes:

> When skies above are dark and grey
> And troubles get you down
> A smile will chase your cares away
> And soon replace your frown.'

It was hardly Shakespeare, concludes Miss Pilgrim, but 'thoroughly typical of Sarah's good-hearted attitude. In the end, she was one of the best headgirls I ever had, as well as being captain of swimming.'

There was more to Fergie than prowess in the pool, however. She was exceptionally kind-hearted and quick to stand up for smaller or weaker girls.

Assistant mistress Anthea Hicks says, 'At the start of Sarah's second term, Flores Belmondo, the daughter of French movie-actor Jean-Paul Belmondo, arrived at the school. She was very homesick, naturally, and her only comfort was a panda called Monsieur Panda. Flores put Monsieur Panda on her bed and then joined the other new girls downstairs for a bedtime cup of hot chocolate. Well, little girls can be very cruel, you know, just as cruel as little boys. When poor Flores went back to the dormitory she discovered that some older girls had cut Monsieur Panda into pieces – distributing his separate parts all over her bed. Flores was distraught, of course, quite stricken, but Sarah, risking the ridicule of the older girls, immediately borrowed a needle and cotton from matron and sewed Monsieur Panda together again. It was a splendid thing to do, and so typical of Sarah.'

Fergie and Flores became inseparable from then on, and lucky Flores will be one of the first to receive an invitation to the royal wedding.

Do blondes have more fun? Yes – when Andy's around! But even at the age of eight, the future Romeo knew how to play hard to get with a mini-skirted lovely around!

It was school chum Flores Belmondo who exerted the greatest influence over the growing Sarah Ferguson during those all-important teenage years.

'They were inseparable,' remembers Susan Caterall, a Hurst Lodge contemporary. 'Flores was a bit younger than Sarah, of course, and utterly different from her – sophisticated, svelte, already very much a young woman of the world – quite prepared to wear make-up and glitter on Speech Day at the ripe old age of fourteen!'

Unlike many of the other girls, Fergie accepted Flores for what she was. 'They made a wonderful couple,' says Susan. 'Sarah was all bounce and laughter, full of that marvellous let's-get-on-with-it quality, and Flores was quiet and devastatingly attractive. They went everywhere together.'

Gallic charmer Flores introduced her freckle-faced friend to a sophisticated world beyond the pony club and the grouse moor.

Perhaps sensing the natural beauty lurking within the shock-haired schoolgirl, Flores insisted that Fergie should have the full run of her extensive wardrobe and make-up box for the annual school dance with boys from the nearby public school, Wellington College.

Friends say innocent young Fergie looked resplendent on the night but for one fashion flaw – she was wearing Flores' suspender belt around her neck!

Andy has always been a determined individualist. He was the first royal to buck tradition by openly eating from a packet of crisps on the royal train. Since the time of Victoria, it had been held to be unseemly for members of the Royal Family to eat while travelling. Nowadays it is commonplace.

Prince Andrew also caused something of a furore in 1977 when he ignored an unspoken family custom by wearing his tie in a Windsor knot. He desisted from this small but significant act of sartorial rebellion only after a heartfelt plea from the Queen Mother.

By the age of fourteen, the young Andy was a keen sportsman, who liked nothing better than to roam his parents' estates with a 12-bore and retriever, doing some 'rough shooting'.

Once his over-enthusiasm for shooting landed him in some right royal trouble. During the cold winter of '76, he shot a swan that had been weakened by the freezing conditions. Andrew later claimed that he mistook the bird for a goose, but the Queen was said to have been mightily displeased with him.

Fact: The swan is known as 'the royal bird'. Ironically, killing one is still punishable by up to seven years' deportation!

'Dying swans' also played a part in the royal-bride-to-be's early days at Hurst Lodge, where she took to ballet in a big way and for a time even hoped to make a career of dancing. When it became obvious, however, that well-built Fergie had outgrown this ambition (she is remembered for her tremendous appetite and was affectionately nicknamed 'Seconds' Ferguson by her schoolmates – always suggesting midnight feasts and fearless when leading raiding parties on the school kitchens!), she became interested in acting and was considered excellent in character parts. Her Cardinal Wolsey in Robert Bolt's *A Man For All Seasons* so impressed Bolt's wife, whacky actress Sarah Miles, that she later sent her son Tom to Hurst Lodge. She also shone as comic servants and Shakespearean clowns.

'Sarah had a terrific sense of humour and frequently had the other girls in fits of laughter,' recalls assistant mistress Miss Hicks. 'She built up a formidable repertoire of impressions, which were funny without being cruel. I gather she still does them, though as the future daughter-in-law of the monarch she may have to cut Mrs Thatcher out of the act and also the Queen Mother, whom she does to a tee, I'm told!'

Another contemporary of Fergie's at Hurst Lodge, writer and actress Joanna Lumley's lively daughter Buzz, remembers that while most of the girls had crushes on pop stars, Fergie was only interested in sportsmen like round-the-world yachtsman Chris Bonington, pentathlete Jim Banks, National Hunt jockey Terry Biddlecombe and racing driver Nelson Piquet.

'She only liked men of action,' says Buzz, 'what she called "real men". She had a huge scrapbook which she filled with photographs of skiers and mountaineers. We used to pull her leg a bit, but she always took our ragging in good part. She was a tremendous sport.'

Unlike his sensitive older brother, Amorous Andy enjoyed his time at Gordonstoun, where he was immensely popular and much admired for his great courage and feats of derring-do on rock face and rugger field.

Jack Cummings, an immediate contemporary of Andrew's and a Perthshire farmer recalls, 'Prince Andrew was always excellent value, always in good heart and determined to be one of the chaps. I remember one long-distance endurance walk we did on a very cold December night. We suddenly realized we had lost a scug – our name for one of the younger boys – somewhere along the way. Andrew insisted on walking back five miles with only his detective for company until they found this boy frozen in a ditch. Even though he was limping himself – he'd twisted his knee quite badly, falling 60 feet down a mountain – he completed the march with the scug on his back, arriving at breakfast time two days later. And, d'you know, he wouldn't have his knee set until the scug had been thawed out in the san. He was impervious to his own pain – almost as if he didn't feel it.'

It was at Gordonstoun that Andrew received a lesson in justice and fair dealing which he has never forgotten.

There was a rule at school which decreed that when bathing in a stretch of river known as Porky's Hole non-swimmers were not allowed to wear trunks.

Although Andrew, a non-swimmer, thought this rule rather harsh, he was determined to be awarded his trunks and would get up very early every morning, go down to Porky's Hole and hurl himself in, only to sink like a stone.

One morning he was surprised to see a senior master, quite naked except for water-wings, being carried to Porky's Hole by Sergeant Buckle, the swimming coach, and thrown in.

'That's fair,' thought Andrew. 'Firm but fair' – and from then on he was determined that any rule that applied to the men applied to the officers too.

The author, wearing the insignia of the order of St George of Gibraltar,
accompanies King Juan Carlos at the passing-out parade at Madrid's
Military Academy.

The royal Prince's fondness for practical jokes was already well in evidence during his time at Gordonstoun.

'He loved throwing things and squirting people with water, and making apple-pie beds and all that kit,' recalls schoolfriend Jamie Scott, now an estate manager in Hampshire, 'but he was always sorry when someone got hurt. I remember one classic joke on the night of Agar's Feast, the highlight of the school year, attended by lots of big wigs and old boys and, on this occasion, by Her Majesty the Queen and Prince Philip and also the German ambassador and his wife. Anyway, Andrew decided to attach cling-wrap to the bowls in the Distinguished Visitors' Lavatory!'

'He also liked to play telephonic jokes on other royals in the middle of the night. He'd ring up the Queen Mum, say, or his cousin Juan Carlos of Spain, and say, "Hullo – I'd like to leave a message for Dick Head." After he'd done this a few times, he'd ring again and say, "Dick Head here. Are there any messages for me?" He was tremendous value. Always on form.'

Fergie's school reports describe her as 'an enthusiastic pupil who makes a cheerful contribution to life at the Lodge'.

Her best subjects were French, English and Modern Dance. She enjoyed music but positively hated maths ('Sarah appears to have no interest whatsoever in the subject and consistently fails to do herself justice in written work').

The report for General Attitude gives a hint of the larger-than-life personality in the making. 'Sarah is lively and full of "go", if a little lacking in direction – but she must learn that liveliness should cease with lights.'

Asked in a Divinity class at Hurst Lodge who was born in a stable and had thousands of followers, Fergie replied, 'Red Rum.'

Andy's tousle-haired temptress once almost trained to be a classical musician! While at Hurst Lodge, she took up the oboe and would practise every day without fail. The budding wind-player was heartbroken when her father, fearful of the effect of *embouchure* on the shape of his lovely daughter's mouth, put a stop to it. Sarah took up the cello but gave it up shortly before her sixteenth birthday.

Although high-spirited Andy surprised his family by getting three 'A' levels at Gordonstoun, these were not of a standard to enable him to follow his older brother to University as a Student Prince!

During an exclusive off-the-record interview with the royal couple, unacademic Andy said, 'I'm sorry I didn't work harder at Gordonstoun, getting good enough 'A' levels to pass into Cambridge, where I would like to have read English. I have recently become very interested in words. Words are very powerful, you know. Even small ones like "if". "If's" a big word in the English language.'

The Sailor Prince then revealed that he had in fact been offered a place at Magdalene College, Cambridge, on leaving school. 'It's a college which still takes a refreshingly unstuffy attitude to academic qualifications,' he said.

'That's right!' bubbled his bride-to-be. 'They throw you a rugger ball and if you catch it they let you in! If you throw it back they give you a scholarship!'

Andrew roared with laughter. 'Whether I'd have passed either test we shall never know!' he joked. 'Within days of the invitation from Magdalene, my father decreed that I should join the Navy immediately.'

Fact: Prince Philip himself never attended University and has argued forcefully against the need for 'excessive higher education'.

Fergie wore braces on her teeth until she was 16. When these were removed she blossomed overnight into the flame-haired beauty with an hour-glass figure we see today – but their removal left her with a slight speech impediment and was unable to say the word 'solicitor' until she was 21. 'She was rather self-conscious about this,' remembers Flores Belmondo, 'and it made her shy with boys. I don't think she had a boyfriend until she could say "solicitor".'

Fergie always had been sensible with money, a quality which must have recommended itself to Her Majesty the Queen, who is known to be thrifty. Once a year at Hurst Lodge fire practice is held involving the Surrey Fire Brigade. After the practice firemen are rewarded with free beer. When the 13-year-old Fergie discovered that the thirsty heroes had drunk a dozen bottles between them she exclaimed, 'Good heavens! I dread to think how many they'd have drunk if there had been a real fire!' The Queen, who once gave each of her staff at Sandringham a pot of chrysanthemums at Christmas with the instruction 'Give the pot back to the gardener when the plant dies', would heartily approve of this attitude.

When she was sixteen, Fergie met the man who was to be one of the greatest influences on her life. Toby Weller Poley. Already a successful businessman, twenty-five year old Weller Poley ('Tobs' to his friends) met schoolgirl Sarah when they were stalking in the Highlands of Scotland.

Something of an intellectual and '*bon viveur*', Weller Poley has remained one of Fergie's closest friends and she is rumoured to have discussed Andy's proposal with him *before* she finally said 'Yes' to her royal suitor.

'It sounds corny', said Weller Poley, 'but we have genuinely been just good friends all this time. I've had some difficult decisions to make and I always valued Sarah's advice before anyone else's – beneath the fun and laughter, she's probably one of the sanest people I know. I'd go to the ends of the earth for her.'

Fergie is also known to hold her friend in the highest esteem. When asked who she would be inviting to the Royal Wedding, she is said to have replied, 'I don't care – so long as Tobs comes.'

After competing in a midnight point-to-point at Cotten-ham, Cambridgeshire, the future Princess Andrew was granted honorary membership of the Dangerous Sports Club, enabling her to wear the coveted DSC badge – a pair of gold, crossed crutches. The only woman in the race, fearless Fergie finished sixth.

While at Lakefield College in Canada, the dare-devil Prince volunteered for what would have been one of the most perilous stunts in royal history. To commemorate the death of Charles Blondin, the legendary equilibrist who crossed Niagara Falls on a tightrope, his grandson, Henri Blondin, planned to repeat the trick pushing a wheelbarrow containing a member of the general public. It was only when the Principal of Lakefield alerted the Palace to the fact that Andrew intended to be the stooge in the wheelbarrow that the stunt was vetoed and another volunteer found.

Despite his lack of enthusiasm as a young lad, the sporting Prince has become the most accomplished shot in the Royal Family. He is estimated to date to have shot over a thousand pheasants, 600 grouse, innumerable pigeons, rabbits and hares, six stags (including a proud 'eleven pointer', one of the best heads in Scotland that year), two wild boar, over 100 snipe (notoriously difficult to shoot), a panther and, as a guest of the Canadian Governor-General, a black bear.

A famous prankster, Andrew has often been accused of 'going too far'. One such occasion occurred a few Christmases ago at Windsor Castle.

It has long been a Yuletide tradition for Her Majesty to put out some miniature stockings full of dog biscuits for her beloved corgis. On this occasion, someone replaced the biscuits with a large number of powerful, chocolate-flavoured laxatives, called Reguletts – with disastrous results!

The finger of suspicion pointed at Andy, but in fact it was Prince Philip who was the joker in the royal pack!

Just like that! Even the crusty Duke cracks up as the star turn in the Royal Crazy Gang goes into his impromptu Tommy Cooper routine.

Answering a ring at her front-door, newly married Princess Anne was surprised to find a gorilla singing 'Happy Birthday To You'. She fetched one of her shotguns and peppered the gorilla as it pedalled away on a bicycle. The surprise had been arranged as a 30th-birthday treat for Princess Anne by her high-spirited brother!

Gorillagram organizer, Mr Harry Meadows, said, 'Princess Anne got off lightly. Our speciality is custard pies.'

On leaving Hurst Lodge. Sarah, who had abandoned any ambition to follow a theatrical career ('Hanging round drafty rehearsal rooms and sharing digs in places like Bristol just wasn't me!' bubbles no-nonsense Fergie), took secretarial and cookery courses, just like any other ambitious teenager, before launching herself into the world. At 18 she landed a job working for Durden-Smith Communications, a Knightsbridge PR company run by Neil Durden-Smith, husband of TV presenter Judith Chalmers. 'She very quickly became an executive secretary,' says Mr Durden-Smith, 52, 'a job with a lot of responsibility, which she thrived on. Sarah's a coper.'

The Romeo Prince has never shared his family's interest in birds – of the feathered variety! at the age of 17, he was sent off to the Seychelles for a fortnight's birdwatching holiday. A few days later, his mother received a postcard, which read:

Dear Ma,

Some puffin here but quite a few shags! Tomorrow we go bird-watching!

love,

Andrew

One of Andrew's closest friends during his formative years was Ferdie Macdonald, now a busy chartered surveyor in Edinburgh. Ferdie, who enjoyed many adventures among the deb set with the happy-go-lucky young prince, has never spoken until now about his royal friend.

'I formed the impression,' says Ferdie, 'that HRH deliberately built up his "Randy Andy" image to punish – if that's not too strong a word – his mother and to find favour with his father. He was perfectly normal, don't get me wrong, no one more normal, but there was an element of play-acting in his relationships with girls. He liked them a lot, but he'd have been as happy, I think, to squirt them with water and throw things at them as to go further, if you known what I mean.'

'I asked him about this once. "Why are you always squirting girls with water, Sir, and throwing things at them?" I said. He seemed baffled. "They like it, don't they?" he said. "When I squirt them with water they squeal. Doesn't that mean they like it?"'

'I think he chose to be a womanizer because there didn't seem to be another available role. Charles was obviously going to be the concerned one – going on about inner-city turmoil and all that kit – and Edward was already showing signs of being a bit of a brainbox. What else could HRH do? I've always felt rather sorry for him to tell the truth.'

Page 7 fella Andy is up early looking for birds – of the feathered variety!
'Some puffin here,' he wrote to the Queen, 'and quite a few shags!'
Her Majesty's response is not recorded!

Whatever the truth of his playboy image, the Royal Romeo relishes the Navy because it treats him as one of the boys, handing out no special privileges because of his status. This is well illustrated by the fact that he was not excused the arduous initiation procedures which every midshipman since the time of Nelson has had to endure before acceptance in the gunroom. Newly commissioned officers are woken at two bells with an icy bucket of water, tossed in a wet sail after a breakfast of vodka and ship's biscuits and then towed behind the ship on a seismic pod – an alarming experience for a non-swimmer like Andrew, but he roared with laughter throughout his ordeal. 'Great bunch of blokes!' he told reporters, as he clambered back on board.

WHOOPS! Absent-minded Andy forgets to wear the rig of the day for morning parade on HMS *Brazen* and is later docked two days shore leave. No royal privileges for the Sailor Prince!

That the Sailor Prince is not in fact a natural womanizer is confirmed by naval chum Lieutenant Harry Hubble, who served with Andrew on HMS *Brazen*.

'I think he found chasing all those leggy models a bit of a strain actually,' says Hubble. 'After a run ashore he'd come back to the mess and tell us about his latest conquest without much joy, as if this sort of thing was expected of him. I think he'd rather have gone out for a jar with his mates to tell you the truth. And he'd often refuse to take a call on the ship-to-shore phone from the latest girl in his life. "For God's sake tell her I'm not here, Harry," he'd say.'

'Even Koo Stark got this treatment on more than one occasion. She'd know he was on board, of course, and she'd curse and swear like a stoker mechanic. Then Andrew would feel sorry. He hates hurting people. That's one of his many splendid qualities. I think Fergie has come as something of a relief, actually. Like slipping into a warm pit after a hairy night on the bridge shipping it green. Fergie's much less demanding, and he was never "out" when she phoned, I can tell you! Fergie's a mate, that's how I see it.'

Page 3 Lovely, Suzi Drew – one of the few busty bomb-shells to 'date' the Playboy Prince without hitting the headlines – further confirms this view of Andrew as a 'reluctant Romeo'.

'There was something vulnerable about him, of the little-boy-lost,' says Suzi thoughtfully. 'I was younger than him, but I often felt more like his older sister, even his mother. Sometimes he'd go very quiet and cuddle up to me, and I'd stroke his head. He was no melon-headed stud, I can tell you. There was nothing he liked more than a Chinese dinner in and then he'd curl up on the sofa with a *Cosmo* quiz – "Are You A Rambo Lover?", "Are You A Wally Or A Winner?", that sort of thing. He'd always fill them in and check his score. Mind you, I knew him before his affair with Koo Stark and I'm told she changed him a lot. For instance, I gather she stopped him referring to making love as "horizontal jogging" – a dreadful expression which always turned me right off. Koo must have taught him a lot. Lucky old Fergie, eh?'

At 21 Sarah left Durden-Smith Communications to zap around America with an old school-chum, Camilla Chamberlain, a great niece of the former Prime Minister.

The two girls had many hilarious adventures, on one occasion losing all their luggage in Baltimore and on another being caught up in a police raid on a brothel in New Orleans, which they had staggered into in a state of exhaustion thinking it was a hotel!

'I was absolutely stunned,' remembers Camilla. 'We were hauled out of bed in the middle of the night by two enormous men in uniform and taken down to the police station, where we were photographed and finger-printed! I was speechless, but Fergie was tremendous and managed to convince them at last that they'd made the most frightful mistake. All the same, it's rather mortifying to think that one's mug-shot will be forevermore on file in a New Orleans police station! And that of the Queen of England's future daughter-in-law too! All good experience, I suppose!'

It was not until she returned from America that full-of-fun Fergie teamed up with her first serious boyfriend, 26-year-old sports-goods salesman, Kim Smith-Bingham. They met, not as has been reported, in Argentina ('Typical of the media to get it all wrong!' says Fergie, who shares her royal fiancé's impatience with inaccurate reporting), but at Klosters, the fashionable Swiss ski resort, where Fergie, always willing to muck in, was working as a chalet girl.

The high-spirited royal-to-be was immediately attracted to Smith-Bingham's sporting prowess and extrovert antics on the slopes.

'Kim had a tremendous sense-of-humour, just like Fergie,' says close friend Charlotte Twohig, 'and he was always making her burst out laughing with his dare-devil escapades. On one classic occasion he went down the Cresta Run on a grand piano and he was always doing totally mad things like attaching cowbells to girls' beds to make sure there was no chalet-hopping!'

Like Fergie, Old Harrovian Smith-Bingham is an accomplished, but never unkind, impressionist and on more than one occasion he'd have his carefree young friends in fits of laughter ordering drinks in a comic German accent or lining up all the waiters in a restaurant and teaching them to sing 'Forty Years On' while he conducted, using a German sausage as a baton!

'Things were never dull when Kim and Fergie were around!' says Charlotte. 'Together they were tremendous value. And yet – somehow one knew it wouldn't last. One always felt that there was something more to Fergie, that she was saving herself for something better, a little less basic.'

The 'something better' to which Charlotte Twohig referred came along in February 1982 in the person of Paddy McNally, race-ace Niki Lauda's former business manager. Fergie met 47-year-old McNally when Smith-Bingham took her to a dinner-party in Verbier, where this quiet, cultured older man has a chalet. She was immediately attracted, perhaps finding this witty, sophisticated man of the world, with his knowledge of furniture and fine wines, a pleasing contrast to the extro-vert Smith-Bingham. She dumped Smith-Bingham on the spot and that night flew with Paddy in Lauda's private jet to Brazil, where the dashing Austrian was to compete in the Brazilian Grand Prix (won, ironically enough, by Sarah's girlhood hero, Nelson Piquet!). 'That's Fergie for you!' the ever-cheerful Smith-Bingham is reported to have said. 'She sees what she wants and goes for it. She's a girl in a million and I wish her all the luck in the world.'

A friend in need . . . One of Jamie Blandford's few real friends, loyal Fergie has stood by the troubled Marquis wherever he happens to be – in the clinic, on bail, in prison, on remand, on probation or on the run.

For the next three years Fergie enjoyed the life of private
jets and Grand Prix, of winters skiing and summers lying
by a pool in Ibiza, where Paddy had a villa half a mile
away from Niki Lauda's. Friends expected the happy-
go-lucky couple to get married but the affair came to an
end for Sarah as suddenly as it had begun. Italian banker's
son Giorgio Paulli, who has lived in Ibiza since 1967,
remembers the occasion well.

'It happened at a lunch party given by Michael
Pearson. Sarah suddenly stood up and said, "This is
leading nowhere! I'm off!" And she walked out. We
never saw her again.'

'Typical of Fergie,' says another close friend, Lulu
Blackwater. 'She was suddenly tired of always being 20
years younger than anyone else in the room. Paddy's
charming, but his friends are all old phoneys and geriatric
playboys like that frightful little man Taki. Fergie
wanted to settle down and have children. I think Paddy
was good for her, though. He taught her a lot. In a way
he was her Koo Stark.'

'Let's face it, Sarah saw things in Ibiza she didn't like,' says Jo Bassett-Turner, a former girlfriend of Jamie, the Marquis of Blandford. 'They're all quite mad out there and on drugs most of the time. Fergie hated all that. She's absolutely genuine, if you know what I mean; what a racehorse trainer would call "honest". Some of the parties were quite wild. She told me about one to which all the men had to come as Adolf Hitler and all the girls as Eva Braun. The party went on all night and at breakfast time they all staggered into Ibiza Town as high as kites. When the local police saw 30 Adolf Hitlers having coffee outside the Montesol they called the German Consul, who had a nervous breakdown.'

Feet-on-the-ground Fergie had seen enough. She packed her bags that morning and flew to London. The incident left her with an abiding hatred of drugs.

'Mind you,' says Jo, 'she's stood by Jamie through all his troubles. That's typical of her. She's one of the few friends he's got. She visits him in prison, in the clinic, on parole, on probation, on remand, on the run – wherever he happens to be at the time.'

The Ferguson family has never believed in the concept of the 'generation gap'. The royal bride's stepmother Sue – Major Ronnie Ferguson's second wife – is a youthful 39. Had Paddy McNally married Sarah, his mother-in-law would have been nine years younger than he was!

Unlike many of her schoolfriends, Have-a-Go Fergie was always determined to pay her own way in the world and, even when her contemporaries were living it up on the deb circuit, did a variety of odd jobs.

'She was incredibly industrious,' remembers Suki Portman, who shared a flat in Kensington with her. 'The rest of us were just zapping around, having tremendous fun but doing not a stroke of work. Not Fergie – she'd be up to all hours at some charity bash, then behind a counter or whatever in the morning. She's quite extraordinary like that!'

And some of the jobs Fergie did at the time were far from glamorous. They included:

SHOP ASSISTANT in Harrods' ski department

COURIER for a firm of travel agents

WAITRESS at Brinkleys' in Chelsea's fashionable Hollywood Road

DRIVER for a friend who cooked directors' lunches

CHALET GIRL in posh ski resorts Murren and Gstaad

GUIDE to the sights of London for groups of American students.

Fact: If Fergie had married ex-sweetheart Paddy McNally, 47, he would have been nine years older than his mother-in-law!

Before her present job, career-girl Fergie was an editor at songsmith Tim Rice's publishing house, Pavilion Books. 'She was damned astute', a colleague remembers. 'All we did in those days were picture books and celebratory volumes of dead film stars by Alexander Walker. Fergie changed all that – the first book she commissioned, in the face of determined opposition in-house, was *Neil's Book of the Dead*. We all thought she was crazy at the time but then *The Young Ones* took off and it turned out to be the biggest seller in Pavilion's history.'

But on-the-move Fergie stayed a mere nine months at Pavilion. 'She was ambitious and there was a certain amount of jealousy here, particularly with her being a woman', commented her former colleague. 'We certainly miss her.'

In November 1984, an unusual incident threw some light on the Prince's extraordinary courage and complete indifference to pain. One evening in Buckingham Palace, he wandered into Prince Charles's quarters, where he found the future king conducting some 'mind over matter' experiments with a group of orange-sheeted Indians – levitating, sitting on hot coals, putting needles through their noses and so forth.

Try-anything-once Andrew joined in and it was soon discovered that he could sit on a lighted gas-ring for longer than the fakirs could. A Harley Street neuro-physiologist was consulted and he diagnosed Smith's Condition. In sufferers from Smith's Condition, signals from different parts of the body reach the brain more slowly than they do in normal people. If a sufferer pricks his finger, for instance, he may not feel anything for as long as five minutes, by which time he has forgotten the incident and he will carry on as if nothing has happened.

In a fit young man, the condition is trivial, manifesting itself in feats of extraordinary courage. In later life, when broken bones should be treated immediately, it is more serious, and it was thought at first that the dare-devil Prince would have to cut out his more hair-raising escapades.

Fortunately, a leading neurophysiologist from Germany was brought in and after further, and much more rigorous tests, it was discovered that Andew didn't suffer from Smith's Condition at all, but was simply quite exceptionally brave.

A little-known side to the Prince's character was revealed during the filming of the German TV documentary series 'Royalty' but cut from the final version at the request of the Palace.

Interviewed on board HMS *Brazen*, the Sailor Prince revealed that, throughout the Falklands War, he carried with him a letter sent to him during his first term at prep school by his beloved royal governess Margaret Curtis (known to the Royal Family as 'Curtie'). Andy declined to show the letter to the German interviewer but explained that it included advice that had stood him in good stead in peace and war throughout his life.

Fact: Until her death in 1977, 'Curtie' lived in a grace-and-favour apartment in the Palace where she was frequently visited by her royal favourite Prince Andrew.

Even in the heat of the Falklands conflict, the world's press never left Prince Andrew's side. Here an Argentinian cameraman yomps with him to Goose Green.

It was after the Falklands War, in the course of which the hero Prince performed his duties with exemplary courage, that his career as a practical joker came to an end.

On 1 April 1983, the high-spirited helicopter ace, who was duty signals officer for the day, sent out the classified 'Scramble' message and put the entire peace-keeping force on a war-footing. Planes took to the air, ships put out to sea without their commanding officers and a platoon of SAS men on the Argentine mainland blew up a power station, plunging Buenos Aires into darkness for 24 hours.

Only the personal intervention of Mrs Thatcher, an ardent admirer of the gutsy Prince, saved him from a serious reprimand. And Prince Philip was said to have warned the Royal Ragger in no uncertain terms that the coveted title of Duke of York would only be his when his Prince of Pranks days were over!

It is not generally known that the Romeo Prince did, in the past, fail to 'hit it off' with some very eligible girls. Among those he rejected, or who rejected him, are:

Joanna Drinkwater (too intellectual)
Carol Thatcher (not intellectual enough)
Selina Scott (too peculiar)
Lulu Birtwhistle (too silly a name)
Lady Teresa Manners (too common)
Princess Melanie Soszynski (Her Majesty's choice, but in love with wet-fish merchant, Henry Root)

And zany TV dancer Leslie Ash, who was chatted up by the Royal Romeo at Peter Stringfellow's society disco until her live-in boyfriend, rubber-faced comedian Rowan Atkinson, dragged her off the dance-floor in a jealous rage. 'Atkinson didn't pull a funny face for a week after the incident,' remarks close friend Humphrey Porter.

If 'Tobs' Weller Poley is Fergie's friend in need, the closest her beloved Andy has come to having a guru is in his surprise relationship with Fleet Street journalist Max Hastings.

The couple met when they were both serving in the Falklands – Andrew as a helicopter pilot and Hastings as a front line war correspondent – and they immediately hit it off. It was Hastings who kept the Prince in touch with developments at home, while grateful Andy returned the favour by ensuring that his new friend's despatches reached London before those of his competitors.

After the conflict was over, the scribe and the sailor kept in touch and on several occasions over the past three years, they have enjoyed each other's company at weekend shooting parties.

'Max has helped Prince Andrew face up to his responsibilities,' comments a Palace insider. 'Unlike Charles's guru Laurens van der Post, he lives in the real world and understands what the Royal Family is all about. He's been a very positive influence.'

In 1984, a man from Leicester put a £50 bet on at Ladbrokes that the christian name of Amorous Andy's next girlfriend would end with an 'i'. The following week, the *Daily Mail* revealed the latest 'raunchy romance of the Romeo Prince – Sandi Jones' – and the lucky punter cleaned up!

Fact: Over 50 per cent of the royal heart-throb's flings have been with girls whose names end with an 'i'.

Stagestruck Sarah's favourite actress is comedienne Felicity Kendal, whom she names as the person she would most like to be if she couldn't be herself. 'I just adore her bubbly sense of fun and the amazingly funny faces she's always pulling!'

It is, in fact, a royal beauty secret that animated Fergie practises Felicity Kendal expressions in the mirror each morning, pulling faces and rolling her eyes – her best features.

Royal beauty secret. Fergie learnt early in life that it's 'P for Personality' that counts! An admirer of TV funny girl Felicity Kendal's bubbly sense of fun, she practises zany expressions in front of the mirror every morning.

It has been estimated that in an average year, Prince Andrew will cover over 450 miles on royal walkabouts and shake 3,980 hands. This compares with his older brother's 320 miles and 2,760 hands and Princess Anne's 690 miles and 7,420 hands.

Despite his cheery, outward-bound image, Prince Andrew has developed a lively interest in books and, whenever his busy lifestyle permits, is never happier than when he is curled up with what he calls 'a rattling good read'.

In 1985, the literary magazine *Book Buyer's Choice* invited him to review a biography of little-known French statesman Talleyrand. As his brief but telling review shows, the bookworm Prince already showed promise as a budding critic:

TALLEYRAND by J. F. Bernard

Biographies are not the most thrilling books. However, every now and then you find one you can't put down. This is one of them. About the great French statesman who survived monarchs and republics, it is amazing to read how – and why – he escaped one side and was accepted by the other. Luck some say, but there is a great deal of luck in life. (There is another study by Duff Cooper but I haven't read it.)

Prince Andrew's literary debut so impressed the editor of *Book Buyer's Choice* – 'I liked his ability to get to the heart of the matter', says editor Liz Thomson – that he was quickly commissioned to write another review. This time it was a spooky thriller that came under the royal gaze:

A FAR CRY by Michael Stewart

Psychiatry, apart from being (a) hard to spell and (b) hard to find in the dictionary to get the correct spelling, is a black art that few understand but rather too many people see. This book intrigued me as I wanted to know more, but the more I was told the less I liked and trusted psyciatrists. On top of this is a fascinating story about a boy afflicted by some terrible trauma. He must find something. Help comes, but . . .

Although the Palace does not officially encourage literary criticism among the royals, believing that their all–important impartiality could be compromised, Andy is determined to contribute the occasional review when he feels he can do something relevant and worthwhile.

Fact: In 1984 Prince Andrew was asked by film producer 'Cubby' Broccoli to screen-test as the new James Bond.

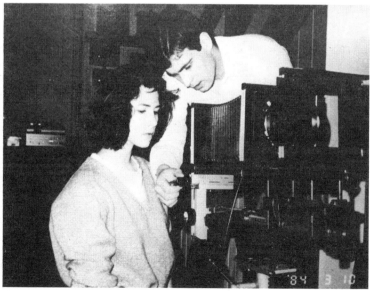

THE PRINCE WITH A PAST

(Top) Sandra – his English rose
(Above) Melinda – she pressed all the right buttons

(Top left) Finola – she danced into his heart
(Top right) Koo – a princely fantasy
(Above left) Katie – the girl next door
(Above right) Vicki – he liked her cheek!

When it comes to navy larks, the game-for-a-laugh Prince is sometimes on the receiving end!

When the *News of the World* columnist Nina Myskow voted Prince Andrew 'Wally of the Week', a daring prankster pinned the offending cutting on the 'Orders for the Day' noticeboard on HMS *Brazen*. But the joke misfired when the amused royal revealed that he didn't know what a 'wally' was!

Prince Andrew resents the fact that he is not allowed to express political opinions. Off the record he divulges that he doesn't favour one political party over another. 'I admire doers and patriots of any political persuasion. They can stretch from those on the extreme right, like Norman Tebbit, clean across the board to people on the extreme left, like David Owen.'

The no-secrets Prince is the only member of the Royal Family to be interviewed by hard-hitting TV personality David Frost.

'Has the attention of the world's press destroyed any candlelit moments?' asked the ex-satirist, referring to the Romeo Prince's much-publicized fling with Koo Stark.

'There are not many candlelit moments to destroy!' was the instant royal riposte.

Andrew's well-chosen words were, six months later, to appear in the American pop charts, having been quoted in a song recorded by Mormon superstar Marie Osmond.

Among the many things that, according to outspoken Andy, 'make my blood boil about the British press is the way it loves to run down our way of life'.

'Take so-called unemployment,' remarked the Prince, 'everyday we hear about it, don't we. Unemployment this, unemployment that – what a ghastly thing it is and all that. But how often do we hear about employment? D'you know something like three times as many people are employed in this country as are unemployed – but we don't hear about them because they're a success and the British press just can't bear success.'

Andrew's 'Pet Hates' include knockers, cynics, talkers rather than doers, and armchair critics.

'We in this country create heroes and then knock them down,' the broad-shouldered young royal told me. 'The people I really admire – Richard Branson, Sir Ian Sinclair, Tim Rice, Michael Grade, Rupert Murdoch, my brother Charles, my father, Prince Philip, Paul Raymonde, my sister Anne, Jeffrey Archer, Ian Botham – have all taken terrific stick from the media. Look what's happening to Ian Botham in the West Indies. Quite appalling.'

The up-and-at-'em young Prince particularly resents the fact that his close friend Mark Thatcher has been forced to join the brain-drain.

'Look at the sniping he took from the media,' continued Andrew. 'Just because he wanted to make some serious money. One sometimes thinks it would serve the knockers right if all our best people packed their bags and left for the States frankly.'

The Prince has a secret passion for Fox's Glacier Mints, which he often sucks to keep his throat clear.

Cheese! The Photographer Prince commemorates the publication of his first book with this self-portrait. He was later to master the complexities of the expensive timing device on his camera.

Frank Robinson, senior cutter at ultra-smart Mayfair hairdressers, Trumpers, visits Prince Andrew to give him a royal trim whenever the globetrotting Prince is in the country. His princess-to-be's locks have been snipped by a number of trendy hair designers – friends say that Fashionable Fergie likes to ring the changes whenever possible!

Fergie is the last in a long line of girlfriends to compliment the Sailor Prince on his absence of side. 'His only vanity,' she says, 'is a slight fear of baldness. I often catch him examining the back of his head in a looking-glass. If he does leave the Navy it will be because having to wear a hat all the time isn't good for his hair.'

It is typical of the 'no side Prince' that he hates the whole subject of class. 'An obsession with class bedevils this country,' he said in an off-the-record interview. 'I blame the lower classes as much as the upper. Both can learn so much from the other. I've learned a tremendous amount from being a Divisional Officer in the Navy. Some of my chaps come to me with the most ghastly problems you could imagine. There's nothing I can do to help, of course, but it's good for them to talk to someone reasonably responsible about it all.'

Fergie's keen sense of humour is already legendary in royal circles – yet the high-spirited princess-to-be understands the responsibilities that go with her position.

When a trainee butler at her father's country home, Dummer Farm, told a distinguished house guest that 'his knickerbockers had been ironed' (he meant plus fours!), it was Fergie who insisted he must go.

Friends say her understanding of protocol and correct form is astonishing for a person of her age.

Following a widely publicized incident when, in a moment of good-natured high spirits, boisterous Andy sprayed paint over members of the American press corps, Mrs Thatcher commissioned a confidential, in-depth viability study from ace ad-men Saatchi and Saatchi with a view to furnishing the Sailor Prince with an entirely new 'toned down' image.

It was one of the PM's rare misjudgements. On being sent the report, the Queen refused to read it. 'I hardly think I need advice on family matters from that frightful little woman,' she is said to have remarked.

Out-front Fergie can be quite a brick-dropper! Failing to recognize socialite Dai Llewellyn at a party, she spent twenty minutes telling him how her friend Vanessa Llewellyn had finaly managed to rid herself of her rude and conceited husband!

On another occasion, she said, 'Weren't you Peter Cook?' to the bemused Sixties satirist.

Doppleganger clanger. Disconsolate actress Joanna Fox is driven home after dinner with 'Prince Andrew'. Pretty Joanna had been romanced by the Royal Romeo's security stand–in – Peter Cousens!

The security risks surrounding the most famous family in the world were highlighted by the attempted kidnapping of Princess Anne in 1974. Since then, Scotland Yard's Special Branch, who are responsible for royal security, have introduced some highly confidential measures to combat the rise in political terrorism.

One of them – the use of identical 'security doubles' as royal stand-ins for high-risk occasions – has backfired in the case of Prince Andrew.

The royal 'twin', a ex-public schoolboy called Peter Cousens, is, say friends, so like his royal boss that even the Prince's Scotland Yard 'minder' Geoffrey Padgham has difficulty telling them apart.

Unfortunately for the Special Branch, the similarity does not end there. Peter has turned out to have a love of life at least equal to that of the royal Prince – in fact, many of the escapades reported as being carried out by Andrew were really perpetrated by his 'twin'.

Among the doppleganger clangers were:

The AFFAIR with nude model Katie Rabbet

The SURPRISE APPEARANCE on stage with raunchy Tina Turner at a benefit concert for mentally handicapped children

The SPANKING INCIDENT at the notorious School Dinners restaurant.

In spite of royal concern, Cousens still works for the all-action Prince – but on a tight leash!

The search for a security double to cover for Fergie started before Andy popped the question! The Special Branch's Superintendent Nevile Bray, who has been responsible for finding lookalikes for the new generation of royals, was said to have reached a shortlist by the end of April.

But the name of the security double, who is 'positively vetted' and who has to sign the Official Secrets Act, is kept a closely guarded royal secret.

Late developer Andy has come a long way since the days
when his father used to refer to him, only half jokingly,
as 'the other one'.

Once a year, the Duke of Edinburgh summons his
royal offspring to his rooms at the Palace for what he calls
his 'annual assessment' – a practice dating from the days
when they were children.

The last 'annual assessment' was said by royal insiders
to have been something of a triumph for Prince Andrew.
His older brother was berated by the crusty Duke for
'having his head in the clouds'. Princess Anne was
warned from being 'too political' and Prince Edward was
told he was 'not getting enough press coverage'.

Only Andrew was passed as having had a 'thoroughly
sound year'.

Absent-minded Andy can't actually remember his first
meeting with his future bride – something irrepressible
Fergie twits him about relentlessly!

In fact, it was at a lunch party at Beaulieu in Hampshire, given by Mrs 'Pussy' Harcourt for her daughter
Camilla.

'He threw a bread-roll at me and I threw it back!'
bubbles full-of-fun Fergie.

The Playful Prince realized at once that she was 'his
sort of girl' and he chased her around the garden!

The Royal sweethearts' love blossomed during Ascot week in June 1985. They quickly discovered that they had many common interests apart from throwing bread rolls. Each, for instance, had seen *Starlight Express* five times.

'I liked her,' says Andy, 'because she's balanced, has both feet on the ground and doesn't go overboard.'

'And nor does he, which is just as well as he can't swim!' bubbles Fergie, bursting into spontaneous laughter.

It is this ability to rag him endlessly which so appeals to the game-for-a-laugh Prince.

By royal standards, Andy and Fergie had something of a whirlwind courtship. Palace-watcher Hugh Egerton-Smyth estimates that they saw each other only 25 times between Royal Ascot and the engagement announcement.

'But it wasn't the breathless romance you read about in the papers,' explains Egerton-Smyth, himself a distant cousin of the Queen. 'They're both sensible, modern young people who know their own minds and believe in getting on with the job in hand. Would there were more like them!'

The Royal Love Birds remember in detail the moment when Amorous Andrew went down on both knees in the romantic setting of Floors Castle, took his love's hand in his and popped the question. Sarah, her mane of red hair spread over her shoulders, blushed and said, 'Yes!'

The historic castle in the Scottish borders, set in 60,000 acres on the banks of the River Tweed and used by Warner Brothers for the Tarzan film *Greystoke*, has long been a sanctuary for love-lorn royals.

In its great halls, draped with the flags and armour of a bygone age, Prince Charles wooed his bride, Lady Diana, and later Andrew dallied with blue-movie actress Koo Stark.

In the last weekend of February, as the rain poured down outside and their hosts, the Duke and Duchess of Roxburghe (family motto – 'Softly Softly Catchee Monkee'), kept discreetly out of the way, the Sailor Prince and the Major's daughter decided to marry.

Sarah had travelled to her assignation in great secret. Even staff at the castle had not been told the identity of the young couple who came to stay. It was only as Sarah slipped back to London that she was spotted leaving Newcastle Airport using the name 'Miss Oxford' – an ironic comment by the irrepressible Major's daughter on the fact that blue-movie actress Koo Stark used to call herself 'Miss Cambridge' when flying to Mustique with her Royal Romeo!

Don't forget the fruitgums, Fergie! Now a member of the Royal Family, Major Ronnie Ferguson still does his shoppng at the village store. 'There's nothing stuffy about Major Ronnie,' says genial shopkeeper, 83-year-old Edith Parker.

The Romantic Royal refuses to be drawn as to what exactly he said to future father-in-law Major Ronnie Ferguson when he drove down to the Ferguson family home to ask for Fergie's hand – but he admits that it was a nerve-racking occasion!

'The Major couldn't have been more kind but I have to admit that it was a hairier experience than flying helicopters in the Falklands!' confesses Andy.

Polo-playing Major Ferguson has taken the royal romance of his beloved Fergie very much in his stride – he's been a royal insider for the past 30 years.

'People will think that I'll change now that I'm a member of the Royal Family,' says the Galloping Major, 'but, at the end of the day, I'll be the same old Major Ronnie that my friends have always known.'

Fact: Major Ferguson has known the royals since the 1950s and, after the break-up of his first marriage, was known to be one of Princess Margaret's favourite escorts.

The Prince of Wales' famous telepathic powers are at their strongest between himself and Andrew, said by Charles to be another 'sensitive'. When the lovestruck Andy rang his older brother to tell him that he had just become engaged, Charles replied, 'I know – I've just heard.'

Asked in the course of an off-the-cuff interview what they least liked about each other, Andrew spoke first, 'I regret to say that Fergie's rather kept up her taste for midnight feasts! She gets up in the middle of the night and comes back to bed with an apple or a bowl of rice crispies. And she's a bit of a grouch in the morning – probably because she's been up half the night raiding the fridge! I tend to be on good form as soon as I leap out of bed, but Fergie won't say a word until she's read the *Daily Mail* from cover to cover.'

'He's *terribly* noisy first thing in the morning!' laughs Fergie. 'He makes *jokes* before breakfast! And he *will* use words that simply aren't on. He must have picked them up in the Navy. Mirror instead of looking-glass, phone, mantelpiece, heads for lavatory – at least he doesn't say toilet!'

Fact: Among the presents Fergie gave her Prince Charming for Christmas 1985 was a copy of *The Complete Naff Guide* by Bryson, Fitzherbert and Legris (Arrow Books, £2.50)!

Watch out, Maggie – there's a Fergie about! The Royal Wedding may have just solved a major headache for Foreign Office bigwigs – what on earth to do about the Falklands?

Following the announcement of the Royal Engagement, Fergie's step-father, polo-playing Argie Hector Barrantes has become something of a media superstar in his homeland Argentina. Now Hector, who speaks English fluently, may be meeting Maggie Thatcher when he flies into London for the big day.

'There's goodwill on both sides,' Hector said in a recent interview on Argentinian television, 'and perhaps a marvellous state occasion like this will get us talking again. Mrs Thatcher is a staunch royalist and I'm sure she would not wish to cast a shadow over this magical moment by taking a hard line over the Malvinas. It would be the icing on the cake.'

A Downing Street spokesman refused to comment on what Foreign Office insiders have already dubbed 'the Fergie initiative'.

Cheers, amigo! Glamorous international playboy Hector Barrantes drinks to the health of his step-daughter Sarah Ferguson between chukkas at the Sporting Club in Buenos Aires. The polo-playing Argie's team lost – a case of Game, Exocet and Match?

A matter of some disappointment to Prince Andrew is the fact that his beloved Fergie has never shared his affection for bluff-talking Max Hastings, whom she finds cold and even slightly pompous. Friends say that Hastings blotted his copybook at a dinner party held at Fergie's Clapham flat when he insisted that the ladies 'retired' while the gentlemen passed the port – a tradition for which thoroughly modern Fergie has no time at all.

The normally good-natured Prince is angered by in-accurate reporting in the media and by the unwritten rule that people in the public eye can't answer back.

'Let's face it, we live in a goldfish bowl,' he says. 'We just have to sit there and take it.'

The Royal Romeo was particularly upset by reports of his nude frolicking on the sun-kissed beaches of Mustique with leggy 'sixties model Vicki Hodge.

'Quite frankly I hadn't even heard of the woman at the time the story appeared in the papers, never mind met her,' he complains. 'And if I had I think I'd have given her rather a wide berth!. One doesn't wish to be ungallant, but – let's face it – she isn't exactly a spring chicken. Funnily enough, I did on a later occasion meet her fiancé, a very sound bloke called Johnny Bindon. He taught me a good trick with a beer mug.'

Andrew lists the worst media offenders as Nigel Dempster, Peter McKay, Richard Compton-Miller, Peter Hillmore and Kenneth Rose.

'Rose once spent a night up a cherry tree outside Koo Stark's bathroom window,' reveals the angry Prince. 'The only gossip writers you can trust are Andrew Morton and Sir Alastair Burnet.'

Yet gallant Andy is more hurt by attacks on his family than on himself. He was particularly upset by whacky satirist Auberon Waugh's description of Captain Mark Phillips as, 'Princess Anne's grinning, speechless husband, who, if you whistle at him, wets himself.'

'Pretty offensive, really, and quite untrue,' says Andrew. 'Captain Phillips can speak as well as you or I. Waugh should get his facts right.'

The chivalrous Prince was also angered by highbrow novelist Penelope Mortimer's biography of the beloved Queen Mum.

'Damned snide actually,' he says. 'Quite frankly I was surprised that such vitriolic stuff should be written by someone who was once married to the creator of the immortal Rumpole of the Baily. He's damn clever, but not too clever, if you know what I mean. He'd never write anything so offensive.'

Fact: Contrary to received opinion, the Royal Family can – and will – sue for libel. Journalist Edward Mylius was given a hefty 12-month jail sentence for libelling George V.

Over the past two years, Andrew's relationship with his older brother Charles has deepened. Friends say that for the first time they are more than just brothers – they're friends, colleagues in the Family Firm.

More than ever, Andy resents the negative publicity that frequently surrounds his thoughtful brother. 'He's really not the nut-chomping loony you read about in the papers,' is his confidential view. 'He spends an awful lot of his own time travelling around the world, drumming up orders for Britain – not the easiest of jobs as you can imagine, given our worldwide reputation for strikes and lost deadlines. He doesn't do it because he likes the sound of his own voice, you know – none of us do it because we like the sound of our own voices.'

The look-you-in-the-eye Prince allows himself a rare flash of anger. 'It's bloody ungrateful. Frankly if every-one worked as hard as my brother does, we wouldn't be in this mess and he wouldn't have to go on about it.'

In spite of her red hair, sunny-natured Fergie seldom loses her temper. The last time anyone can remember her becoming angry was during the televised engagement interview when she was asked whether her uncle, Major Brian Wright, who is a butler for the Cavendish family at Holker Hall in Cumbria, would be invited to the royal wedding. Down-to-earth Fergie, who hates snobbishness of any sort, exploded, 'Of course he'll be invited. How absurd! But he'll know the form well enough not to come.' The exchange was edited out of the interview so viewers missed the chance of seeing the flame-haired royal-to-be in a right royal paddy!

The royal couple share a love of good books. Fergie reads a lot when she has the time, but 'nothing madly intellectual, nothing artsy-fartsy'. Her favourite authors include Jilly Cooper, Dick Francis, Dirk Bogarde and Claire Francis.

'They don't write as if they've swallowed the dictionary,' says Fergie.

She also admires journalists Jean Rook and Lynda Lee-Potter. 'They cut through all the waffle and get to the point,' she enthuses.

Her fiancé's favorite authors are Jeffrey Archer, Tom Sharp and Alastair Maclean.

'Which one of you lot's the Sugar Plum Fairy?' quipped the Prince of Patter during a surprise visit backstage at the Royal Opera House. The delighted artistes roared with laughter. 'Takes one to know one,' riposted *danceur noble* Anthony Dowell.

Bubbly Sarah's sense of humour is similar to Andrew's, if a trifle more subtle, thanks to the time she spent with Paddy McNally. Her favourite comedians are Kenneth Williams and Peter Bowles – his are Peter Cook and Dudley Moore – and she likes sophisticated sit-coms such as 'To The Manor Born', 'The Good Life', 'Robin's Nest' and 'Yes Minister' ('*So* accurate!') and 'absolutely anything with Maureen Lipman'.

'And who's that fat man who's *always* on the box?' asked Fergie. 'I adore his quick-fire cracks. *You* know, bald, Australian . . .'

Her Sailor Prince was quick to help her out. 'Clive James, sausage!' he laughed.

Palace insiders still cringe at the memory of dishy Di's entrée into the royal circle. Today the Princess is the perfect royal, but then she did EVERYTHING wrong!

DI'S BLOOMERS...

LISTENING to a Sony Walkman on Remembrance Sunday at the Cenotaph and tapping her foot during the one minute's silence

BREAKING time-honoured royal protocol by referring to royal retainers at the Palace as 'servants' –they are *always* known as 'staff'

TURNING her back on the Queen

PLONKING herself down on Prince Charles's lap during a family evening at Balmoral

REFUSING to eat alone with the Queen because 'they had nothing in common'

MIMING for a royal game of charades 'No Sex Please – We're British'

FAILING to recognize Mrs Thatcher at a public function

INTRODUCING François Mitterand to a waxwork of the Queen at a reception held at Madame Tussaud's – it was 10 minutes before the French President, still talking animatedly to the dummy, was 'rescued' by one of his staff

CALLING a huntsman wearing hunting pink 'a redcoat'

Described by Palace protocol chiefs as 'an apt pupil', Fergie will no doubt learn from Di's chequered career as a thoroughly modern royal.

Fergie's reputation as a royal rib-tickler has already landed her in a spot of bother at the Palace.

When, during the autumn of 1985, the Royal Love Birds paid a visit to the Queen in her rooms at Buckingham Palace, they were greeted by Her Majesty, wearing a dressing-gown, slippers – and her crown!

Sensing a practical joke, saucy Sarah hooted with good-natured laughter.

She was later informed by her famous fiancé that her levity was misplaced. During the week before the State Opening of Parliament. the Queen likes to get accustomed to her weighty crown by wearing it every day around the house.

Initially put out by her future daughter-in-law's ill-timed guffaws, Her Majesty later took Fergie's *faux pas* in good part.

Asked what he believes he and Fergie contribute most usefully to the British way of life, the straight-as-a-die Prince gives a no-nonsense response.

'I've always believed that my greatest asset as a member of my family was the fact that I really am a very straight-forward sort of chap, and I'm sure Sarah will be with me all the way here. We're just a perfectly normal couple setting up home together – we both know lots of people exactly like us.'

And the royal couple have a refreshingly feet-on-the-ground attitude when it comes to bringing up children. Says Andy, 'When we have a son, I'd like him to have an entirely normal life just like me.'

Game-for-a-laugh Fergie can always take a joke against herself. When zany puppeteers Fluck and Law added her to their cast of characters in *Spitting Image*, Fergie led the laughter. Two days later, Fluck and Law were delighted to receive a personal letter, signed by Fergie's new secretary Wing Commander Adam Wise, enquiring as to the availability of the original model.

Visitors to Andy and Fergie's new home will now be confronted by a life-sized Fergie in the royal smallest room. Should they get over the shock of that, they will be further inconvenienced by a musical toilet roll which plays 'God Save The Queen' – one of zany Andy's most prized possessions!

Fergie is a thoroughly modern girl – equally at home on grouse moor or in a fashionable disco – but she's no humourless women's libber. She sees a woman's role as essentially that of back-up.

'We're a team,' she says, 'but the man must be on the bridge. He's the captain, I'm the first lieutenant.'

Insiders point out, however, that strong-willed Fergie will be no doormat. She's very protective towards her easy-going husband-to-be and believes that many of his past girlfriends – whom she refers to privately as 'Andy's tarts' – were simply taking advantage of his trusting nature to advance their own dubious careers.

Between now and the royal wedding, Britain's best-known bride-to-be will undergo the customary eight-week crash course at Buckingham Palace in how to become a royal. Fergie, unlike her Palace pal, the rebellious Lady Di, who had to take the course twice before passing, is expected to do splendidly. The course is supervised by the Queen Mother and includes instruction on royal quips and patter, how to chat informally and burst out laughing, how to shake hands with black Commonwealth leaders and how to freeze outsiders who make jokes involving a knowledge of Anthony Powell's novels.

'The Look'
There are two sides to her Majesty – the woman who has been known to
perch on a chair munching a Mars bar, and the monarch who, when
displeased by over-familiarity or a breach of etiquette, can freeze her victim
with 'the Look', famous in Court circles and never forgotten by the
unfortunate recipient. But which of the Royals has mastered 'the Look'?
(Above) The Look: RIGHT

The Look: WRONG

The Look: RIGHT

The Look: WRONG

The Look: ALMOST . . .

The Look: RIGHT – At the age of seven, Fergie (left) shows she's got what it takes to be a Royal!

Fergie's greatest influence as to the Rights and Wrongs of Court life will almost certainly be Britain's loveliest royal, Princess Michael.

The Princess, despite her relative inexperience, has an instinctive knowledge of correct form and civilized behaviour.

'She's a natural,' says Palace-watcher Sir Alastair Burnet. 'While there's always something slightly contrived about Di's efforts to be nice, Princess Michael puts everyone at ease without appearing *too* relaxed. If Fergie's looking for a royal role model, it has to be Princess Michael.'

In the run-up to the wedding for which all the world is waiting, famed drama-coach, Tutti Lenya, has had to work overtime teaching sweet-natured Fergie 'the look' – the Gorgon-glance that royals can direct at over-familiar outsiders with the force of an ice-pick in the forehead.

'I have been teaching 'the look' to members of the Royal Family for 30 years,' says Miss Lenya, who, as an ex-method actress makes her distinguished pupils imagine they are confined in a cupboard with a gas-leak and a crate of kippers. 'The Queen and Princess Anne needed no coaching. Some of the naturally nice royals, such as Princess Alexandra and the Duchess of Kent, presented difficulties, but Sarah has been a special problem. She really lacks an unpleasant streak, and I fear she may never master "the Look".'

Fact: Fergie is said to have been particularly impressed by her future brother-in-law, Charles's advice for royal absolute beginners, 'Never remind people who you are – until they forget.'

Life as a royal has its snags, as its newest recruit soon discovered. Many of the things that a normal youngster of her age might take for granted were, Fergie was told, strictly 'off limits' for a future member of the Family Firm.

OUT went the top of the range BMW which tearaway girl-about-town Fergie had just bought

IN came a suitably British but *second-hand* Jaguar XJS taken from the Palace fleet

OUT went Fergie's nights on the town -- dinner at the ultra-posh Le Gavroche, dancing with the deb set at Annabels, rounded off with a Bucks Fizz and kedgeree breakfast at the Ritz

IN came an energy-sapping round of social functions and charity balls – Andy's bubbly beauty is suddenly on everybody's list!

OUT went carefree last-minute jaunts to Paris, Rome or Gstaad in a pal's private jet

IN came a carefully planned schedule of tough, business-before-pleasure royal tours

As a token of her regard for her future daughter-in-law, the Queen has agreed that her own private dresser, Miss 'Bobo' Macdonald, may prepare the fairy-tale Princess for the royal wedding.

Miss Macdonald, a Scottish woman of humble birth, has been with Her Majesty for over 50 years and has not set foot outside the Palace since 1956. As well as advising 'The Little Lady' – her name for the Queen – on matters of dress, she is said to have influenced her royal employer on many matters of state on occasions when Her Majesty seeks a 'view from the street'.

Fact: Princess Diana was obliged to use her own 'dresser' for the last royal wedding.

Sparky Sarah causes a bit of a problem when it comes to designing dresses for her. She's electrical – literally! For our newest royal is what milliners call 'a clinger'. Her body generates so much static electricity that the favoured materials – silk, crêpe de chine and chiffon – have a tendency to cling to the contours of her body. A lining of organza is sometimes used to reduce the electrical charge.

Watt a poser for the royal designers!

A '*vendeuse*' from the famous House of Hartnell had one word for our newest Princess after a fitting for a going-away-dress – radiant!

She's totally natural,' said Katherine Fox. 'After meeting her, you feel as if you've had a tonic – It's like you've just been on holiday for a fortnight!'

The Royal Twosome may raise a glass on the big day – but the bubbles will be from Perrier water! For, in spite of their life-in-the-fast-lane image, the Love Birds share a distaste for alcohol.

It was at her first grown-up party that teenage tippler Fergie discovered her remarkably low tolerance for the demon drink. Friends at the party say that the royal-to-be was no 'wilder' than her normal self but the next day's king-size hangover told its own story!

Prince Andrew's first and last serious taste of alcohol was at an end-of-term binge at Gordonstoun, since when he has been almost entirely teetotal – in fact, wags on HMS *Brazen* dubbed him 'the ginless wonder'!

Who will take the royal wedding photos now that photographer-in-waiting Lord Lichfield has been ruled out following kiss-and-tell revelations by topless model Suzi Drew?

Andrew's suggestion that he should take them himself using an expensive new Japanese timing device has been ruled out by Palace officials. At Charles and Diana's wedding, the photographer Prince had used a similar device – with disastrous results. The pictures revealed nothing but waiters clearing up the reception room and the Duchess of Munster stuffing smoked salmon sandwiches into her handbag.

TOP SECRET! Special Branch graphologist Sergeant Dermot Smythe's analysis of Fergie's handwriting – part of the Branch's highly confidential Positive Vetting routine – reveals that she's the perfect princess.

The sergeant's verdict? Loyal, good-natured and with a zany sense of fun. No problems!

Like Charles and Di, the Royal Love Birds will be leaving a list of suitable wedding presents at Sloane Street's ultrasmart department store, the General Trading Company – but Sensible Sarah will be avoiding the errors that her Palace Pal made!

On returning from their honeymoon, the Prince and Princess of Wales discovered that they had no less than NINE Royal Doulton dinner sets, SEVEN sets of cut-glass wine goblets, SIXTEEN candelabras and TWO pianos, but NO kitchen utensils with which to cook the first royal meal *à deux*.

Practical Fergie has included on her list: frying pans (3), spatulas (2), washing-up clothes (10), colander (1), teasmade (1), toasters (2), floor squeezies (3) and Hoovers (2).

Di and Andy share a quiet word at Royal Ascot. Always close, the
non-riding Palace Pals now have something else in common – they're both
hitched to horse-lovers!

It is Palace protocol never to employ married women –
and the royal couple will be required to obey this
unwritten rule when they set up home together.

Doubtless tender-hearted Fergie will take a leaf out of
her mother-in-law's book when it comes to letting go a
female member of staff who has decided to get married.

To avoid embarrassing personal appeals, Her Majesty
goes for a long walk with the corgis until it is all over.

Andy and Fergie's frank affection for his controversial
aunt, Princess Margaret, is, according to royal insiders, a
source of great comfort to the Queen's sister.

Sad Margaret's increasing estrangement from the
Palace has been accelerated by the sharp decline in her
relations with Charles and Di. Friends say that the
trouble started during the last royal engagement when
Charles took his bride-to-be to dinner with larger-than-
life Margaret. Di, ever anxious to please, had been
warned that Charles's high-spirited aunt loved to do
impressions and was hurt if no one appreciated them.

Early in the dinner, Margaret made a comment and,
sensing a zany impression, Di burst into peels of un-
restrained laughter. Unfortunately Princess Margaret
was speaking in her normal voice.

The royal couple have not been invited back to
Princess Margaret's apartment at Kensington Palace to
this day.

Play-fair Fergie has insisted that none of the vulgarity that surrounded the wedding of her Palace Pal Princess Di will be repeated on her own Big Day. So it was:

NO to plans to open the Fergie family home in Dummer to tourists once a week

YES to the idea of a new ten-foot high wall, constructed from traditional Hampshire brick, to ensure privacy for the family

NO NO to the proposal that Andy and Fergie should make a pre-wedding royal video to stimulate interest in the event throughout the Commonwealth

YES YES to the banning of all Royal Love Bird memorabilia except for headscarves sold through the top people's store Harrods and Talbot Church's Royal Love Bird T-shirt Offer

NO NO NO to wedding invitations for zany trend-setters Bob Geldof, Charlie Nicholas and Rik Mayall

YES YES YES to established royal showbiz favourites Elton John, Paul Eddington and Phil Collins.

Like every young bride, no-nonsense Fergie has doubtless asked herself what marriage guidance experts call 'the Big Question': 'Will I get on with my mother-in-law?'

In fact, as my exclusive survey reveals, the easygoing Princess will need all of her famous charm and tact to avoid potential trouble spots.

In the interest of royal harmony, here are some subjects Fergie would be well advised to avoid:

PETS The Queen hates cats. Fergie loves them.

FOOD The only dessert the Queen will ever eat is a small helping of Christmas pudding. Fergie is notorious for her sweet tooth!

MONEY The Queen's thriftiness is legendary – she checks her share portfolio in the *Financial Times* even before she reaches *Sporting Life*. Fergie's motto could well be 'If you've got it, flaunt it!'

ASTROLOGY The Queen is a firm believer in the stars. Fergie calls it 'bilge' ('We're very sceptical, we Librans,' she says).

AMERICANS Like her husband, the Queen regards contact with 'our American cousins' as one of her most irksome chores. Fergie once went out with an American.

FLOWERS The Queen's favourite flower is the carnation. Fergie likes bluebells.

PRINCESS MARGARET The Queen sees sad Margaret as rarely as possible. Both Andy and Fergie like nothing better than to spend an evening with his fun-loving aunt.

CARS Since her wartime stint in the ATS, the Queen has a detailed knowledge of mechanics and takes a keen interest in motor-car engines. Fergie couldn't care less about what goes on under the bonnet – just so long as it goes!

MUSIC The Queen refuses to go anywhere without listening to her favourite military band music on the cassette machine in her Rolls-Royce. Thoroughly modern Fergie likes Dire Straits, Neil Diamond, Elton John and the occasional popular classic.

HEIGHTS The Queen is afraid of heights. Action-woman Fergie is not.

The publican who tried to buy the Green Hand pub in Fergie's home village of Dummer shortly after the announcement of the Royal Engagement might have had a shock if his cash-in-quick ploy had paid off. Because, despite Fergie's instant popularity as the girl-next-door royal, the village has NOT been inundated with rubber-necking tourists, as was widely forecast.

A local shopkeeper Peter Smedley commented, 'We were expecting coachloads but frankly, apart from a couple of Sunday drivers from Basingstoke, it's been like a morgue round here. We've sold one Royal Love Bird souvenir mug and that's your lot.'

The mercenary Mr Smedley has been confounded by the traditional British respect for privacy – even for Royals!

Fairy-tale Princess greets 'Wicked Stepmother'! Irreverent Sarah often refers to Susan Ferguson as 'my wicked stepmother' but good sport Susan takes it all in good part.

There's nothing stuffy about frisky Fergie, say Palace insiders. Although a firm believer in protocol, she's quite prepared to bend the rules when she finds them ridiculously old-fashioned.

For example, according to time-honoured royal tradition, her father should bow to her and call her 'Ma'am'. Fergie realizes that it is an absurd rule for close family.

So when she's with Major Ronnie behind Palace walls, she simply doesn't bother. However, when they meet in public, the apprentice princess insists on the formalities.

And the second Mrs Ferguson is required to call her famous stepdaughter 'Ma'am' at all times.

Her relationship with collector Paddy McNally has helped to give Fergie a lifelong love of art. A connoisseur of contemporary sculpture, she has one of the largest collections of sporting bronzes in this country.

Her favourite sculptor, former ace National Hunt jockey Philip Blacker, has become a personal friend of the royal couple and is rumoured to have been commissioned by McNally to complete a new racing bronze 'Coming From Behind' in time for the wedding.

The Patient Prince is made angry by suggestions that he is somehow insulated from real life, that he and other royals are merely participants in some glorified soap opera.

'I've been towed at 30 knots on a seismic pod, shot at by brother Argie, dropped out of aeroplanes, had an affair with Koo Stark,' expostulates the dare-devil Prince. 'I'd like to see a Hollywood actor do some of the things I've done!'

Andrew's favourite word is 'bonce'.

His favourite historical characters are Nelson, Henry V, Albert Schweitzer, Cecil Rhodes and Martin Luther King.

His favourite meal is breakfast.

Fergie's favourite words are 'today', 'cope' and 'now'. Her favourite expression is 'Let's get on with it'. Her least favourite words are 'can't', 'tomorrow', 'chairperson' and 'yesterday'.

Her favourite colour is red.

Her favourite film stars are Meryl Streep, Robert de Niro and Al Pacino.

Her favourite newscaster is Sandy Gall.

RULES OF ENGAGEMENT – THE KISS THE WORLD WAS
WAITING FOR. (Above) Chocks away . . .

(Top) Lift-off...
(Above) Fully engaged!

It's the wedding invitation the world is waiting for!

A privileged glimpse at the Royal Love Birds' draft guest list suggests there will be joy and disappointment in the coming weeks.

So – come the Big Day – Who'll be IN and who'll be OUT?

IN	OUT
The Duke of Beaufort	The Duke of Devonshire
Lady Camilla Dempster	Nigel Dempster
Peter Townend	Betty Kenward
Koo Stark	Vicki Hodge
Talbot Church	Godfrey Talbot
Anne Beckwith-Smith	Carolyn Beckwith-Smith
The Duke of Argyll	Margaret, Duchess of Argyll
Lord Delfont	Lord Weidenfeld
Lady Fermoy	Viscountess Rothermere
Lady Antonia Fraser	Norman St John Stevas
King Hussein of Jordan	The Aga Khan
Sandy Gall	Sir Alastair Burnet
James Whitaker	Geoffrey Wheatcroft
Harry Evans	Tina Brown
William Hickey	Kenneth Rose
Jilly (and Leo) Cooper	The Krankies
Major Ronnie Wallace	Wayne Sleep
Nick and Judy Gaselee	'Jinx' Jenkins
Julie Burchill	Nicholas Coleridge
Steve Cauthen	Willy Carson
Bruce Oldfield	David and Elizabeth Emanuel
Henry Root	Richard Ingrams
Henry Porter	Peter Hillmore
'Tobs' Weller Poley	Lord Lichfield
Joanna Drinkwater	David Litchfield
Carolyn Herbert	Liz Brewer
Max Hastings	Sir David English
'Buzz' Lumley	Karen Stringfellow

IN	OUT
Debbie Raymonde	Paul Raymonde
Sir Harry Secombe	Spike Milligan
Phil Collins	Bob Geldof
Paula Yates	Janet Street-Porter
Michael Clayton	Lucinda Green
Felicity Kendal	Tracey Ullman
Paul Eddington	Tom Bell
Lady Edith Foxwell	Lady Melchett
All Guinesses (except Daphne)	All Shand-Kydds
Jamie Blandford (if out)	Taki Theodoracopulos (unless in)

Now Available

A full range of Talbot Church's Royal Love Bird Tee-shirts is now available. Details from:

Royal Offer
Church House
91 Wendell Road
London W12 9SB

Picture Acknowledgements

Cover photograph: Julian Parker/Frank Spooner Pictures
Pages 9 and 15: Popperfoto
Page 23: John Scott/Camera Press
Pages 31, 39 and 43: Rex Features
Page 45: Syndication International
Pages 51 and 55: Alan Davidson/Alpha
Page 59: Michael Charity/Camera Press
Page 63 (both): Alan Davidson/Alpha
Page 66 (above): John Scott/Camera Press
Page 66 (below): Alpha
Page 67 (top left) David Parker/Alpha/Camera Press
Page 67 (top right) Catherine Ashmore/Camera Press
Page 67 (bottom left) Press Association
Page 67 (bottom right) Alan Davidson/Camera Press
Page 71: Popperfoto
Page 75: Press Association
Page 81: Rex Features
Page 85: Press Association
Page 91: Syndication International
Page 98: Lionel Cherruault/Camera Press
Page 99: Jim Bennett/Alpha
Page 100: Rex Features
Page 101: Popperfoto
Page 102: Fernand Gutterrez/Camera Press
Page 103: Desmond O'Neill
Page 109: Syndication International
Page 111: Press Association
Page 117: Syndication International
Pages 122-3 (all): Ian Swift/Camera Press